# Awesome Fashion

## Coloring Book for Stylish Girls

# Welcome!

Step into a world of stunning fashion for
every girl and occasion!

This is where it all starts! Get ready for a stylish
adventure through the seasons: from spring florals to
cozy winter looks, sporty days, country chic,
party fun, and many more!

Each chapter is suitable for different ages, from
youngest to oldest, making it easy to find the perfect
looks. Try to recreate your own style as you explore
this coloring activity. Let's jump into fashion fun!

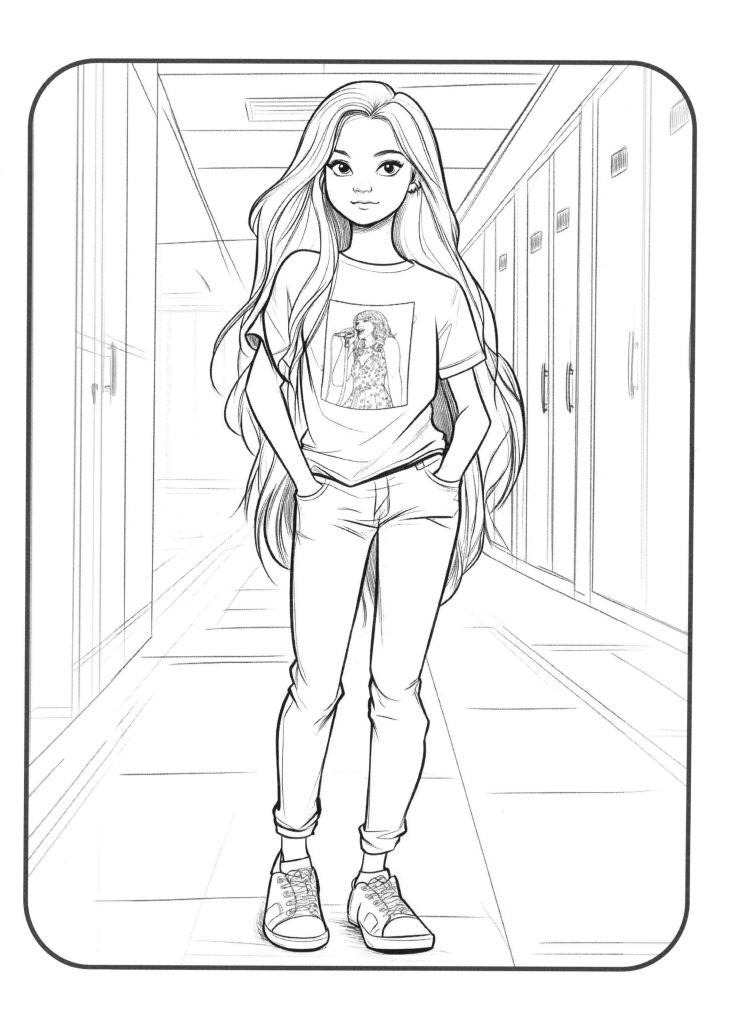

# Spring Splendor

Spring has sprung, and so has the fashion!
This chapter is all about fresh colors, floral
prints, and that perfect touch of sunshine.

Whether you're dreaming of twirling in a
flowy dress or kicking back in comfy, springy
layers, we've got you covered.

Time to let your wardrobe blossom as
beautifully as the flowers!

# Sunlit Chic

Grab your sunglasses and flip-flops because it's summer time! In this chapter, we bring you all the best looks for those sunny beach days, summer festivals, and outdoor adventures.

From breezy dresses to cool shorts and sandals, we've got everything you need to stay chic and comfy in the summer heat.

Let's make this summer
the most stylish one yet!

# Autumn Allure

Autumn is here, and it's time to cozy up in the latest fall trends. Think warm tones, soft scarves, and boots perfect for crunching through leaves.

Whether you're heading back to school or just soaking in the crisp air, this chapter brings all the cozy vibes you need to look and feel your best.

Let's fall in love with autumn style!

# Frosted Glam

Winter has arrived, and with it, the coolest (and warmest!) outfits. From cute coats to fuzzy boots, this chapter is all about keeping cozy while looking oh-so-chic.

Whether you're building snowmen, sipping hot chocolate, or just enjoying the frosty days, we've got the perfect winter wardrobe ideas to keep you snug and stylish all season long!

# In the Country

Yeehaw! It's time to bring some country
charm into your closet. This chapter is all
about denim, plaid, and those cute
country-inspired outfits that are perfect for
every outdoor adventure.

Whether you're dreaming of a farm day or
just love the rustic look, you'll find everything
you need to feel country-fabulous. Let's
saddle up for style!

# Sporty Look

Are you ready to move? This chapter is packed with outfits perfect for staying active while looking awesome.

Whether you're hitting the field, the track, or just hanging out in your favorite sporty gear, this collection will keep you looking cool and feeling comfortable.

Let's get sporty in style!

# Creative Couture

Get creative with your fashion in this artsy chapter! From bold patterns to fun accessories, we've got the outfits that let you express your unique style.

Whether you're painting, crafting, or just adding some creative flair to your day, these looks are all about letting your imagination run wild.

Time to bring out your inner artist dnd shine!

# Bestie Chic

What's better than sharing great moments with your besties? Sharing great style! This chapter is all about fun looks you and your BFFs will love.

Whether it's matching outfits or coordinating pieces that show off your friendship, we've got everything to make your fashion game strong together.

Time to dress up and make memories with your besties!

# Party Perfection

It's party time, and that means
it's time to dress to impress!

Whether it's a birthday bash, a school dance,
or a fun get-together, this chapter is packed
with show-stopping outfits that will make you
feel like the star of the night.

Get ready to shine, sparkle, and have a blast
in your perfect party look!

Congratulations, young fashionista!
You've brought life to every page with
your vibrant colors and stylistic choices.

This certificate is a testament to your
talent and artistic spirit. Well done!

This certificate is awarded to:

Thank you for joining us on this colorful journey!
We hope your little artist had a blast. If you enjoyed the adventure,
we'd be grateful for a review on Amazon.

Your feedback helps us create more delightful experiences!

Made in United States
Orlando, FL
08 December 2024

55216648R00048